12 WAYS TO IMPROVE
ATHLETIC PERFORMANCE

by Todd Kortemeier

www.12StoryLibrary.com

12-Story Library is an imprint of Peterson Publishing Company and Press Room Editions.

Produced for 12-Story Library by Red Line Editorial

Photographs ©: Vadim Martynenko/Shutterstock Images, cover, 1; Susan Chiang/iStockphoto, 4, 15, 24; gbh007/iStockphoto, 5, 12, 29; joebelanger/iStockphoto, 6; Roberto A Sanchez/iStockphoto, 7; pookpiik/iStockphoto, 8; leezsnow/iStockphoto, 9; digitalskillet/iStockphoto, 10; monkeybusinessimages/iStockphoto, 11; 4kodiak/iStockphoto, 13; Christopher Futcher/iStockphoto, 14, 19, 27; Sasha Samardzija/Shutterstock Images, 16; ArtBoyMB/iStockphoto, 17; Lisa Thornberg/iStockphoto, 18; ActionPics/iStockphoto, 20, 28; Spotmatik/iStockphoto, 21; Prykhodov/iStockphoto, 22; Digital Vision./Photodisc/Thinkstock, 23; Okea/iStockphoto, 25; John Storey/2K SPORTS/AP Images, 26

Library of Congress Cataloging-in-Publication Data
Cataloging-in-publication information is on file with the Library of Congress.
978-1-63235-369-6 (hardcover)
978-1-63235-387-0 (paperback)
978-1-62143-511-2 (hosted ebook)

Printed in the United States of America
Mankato, MN
May, 2016

Access free, up-to-date content on this topic plus a full digital version of this book. Scan the QR code on page 31 or use your school's login at 12StoryLibrary.com.

Table of Contents

Warm-Ups Are the Way to Start

Playing in games is fun. But practice is where you get better. Practice helps you get ready to play your best. In a similar way, a warm-up routine is important. It can be a great start to any workout, practice, or game.

A warm-up gets your blood flowing. It also makes your body temperature rise. When your muscles are warm, you won't feel as sore after working out. Also, you may be at a lower risk of injury. Increased blood flow reduces strain on muscles. A warm-up should be similar to the activity you're about to do. But it should be slower.

Stretching after a warm-up can help reduce the risk of injury.

Jogging is one example of a warm-up.

A warm-up should make you break a sweat. It shouldn't leave you tired, though. Doing some stretches can be helpful, too. But always stretch after the warm-up. Stretching cold muscles can lead to injury.

The partner to a good warm-up is a cooldown. This comes after the activity. A cooldown is a less intense version of the sport you just played. For instance, suppose you were running. As a cooldown, take a walk for five to 10 minutes. This helps your heart rate and body temperature steadily return to normal. Stopping exercise too quickly could leave you feeling dizzy.

120
Maximum heartbeats per minute when it's safe to stop cooling down.

- Warm-ups prepare you to be in the best shape to compete.
- They also can help reduce injury.
- A warm-up is a less intense version of the activity you're about to do.
- A similar cooldown should follow any exercise.

THINK ABOUT IT
There is a mental side to sports, too. What are some good ways to mentally prepare to play a game?

2

Playing Multiple Sports Has Benefits

The more you practice a sport, the better you get at it. But that doesn't mean you should focus on just one sport. In fact, there are benefits to playing multiple sports.

Trying more sports helps you figure out what you like. It's important to love the game you play. But playing too competitively can take the focus away from developing skills.

Many sports have skills in common. So the skills you gain in one sport can be useful in other sports.

For example, Alisa Camplin trained as a gymnast. But she later used that strength and flexibility in another sport. She became an Olympic gold medalist in skiing.

Playing multiple sports also helps prevent injuries. Many sports have motions that players do over and over again. Repetitive motions can lead to injury. This is especially true for kids who are still growing. Consider waiting until after your 12th birthday to focus on one sport. Studies show you will have a better chance of success.

It's a good idea to try lots of sports just for fun.

Pitching a baseball is a repetitive motion.

MULTI-SPORT ATHLETES

Bo Jackson and Deion Sanders are two of the best multi-sport athletes ever. Both played pro football and pro baseball. In football, Jackson made the Pro Bowl as a member of the Los Angeles Raiders. In baseball, he was an All-Star with the Kansas City Royals. Sanders is the only athlete to play in both the Super Bowl and World Series. He is in the Pro Football Hall of Fame.

16

Maximum number of hours an athlete should train per week. Any more has a higher risk of injury.

- Playing multiple sports helps athletes choose the right one for them.
- They also develop a wider range of skills.
- A lack of repetitive motion from one sport helps an athlete avoid injury.
- Avoid choosing just one sport until at least age 12.

3

Weight Training Builds Strength

Weight training has many health benefits. It can also help improve athletic performance. Lifting weights builds strength by making your muscles work. Gradually adding more weight helps your muscles grow stronger.

Many sports depend on power from the legs. Weight training can help athletes run faster and jump higher. One common lift is called a squat. An athlete puts weight on the shoulders. Then she lifts with the legs.

It's also important to use motion in weight training. This prepares the body for many types of activity. One lift that has many motions is called the clean and jerk. This lift involves the legs, arms, and wrists. An athlete raises a bar from the ground to above the head. The clean and jerk works many different types of muscles.

Be careful when starting a weight program. Do a proper warm-up. Don't lift more than you can

Always make sure your weights are the right size for you.

handle. And check with an expert to make sure you're using good form. This will help you avoid injuries.

Weight training should also include variety. Don't work the same muscle groups two days in a row. That will cause the muscles to be overworked. And remember that your focus should be strength, not just building muscle. Flexibility and movement are keys to improving athletic performance. Too much weight training may harm that.

8

Age you should be before starting any kind of weight training program.

- Weight training builds strength that improves performance.
- Gradually lifting heavier weights builds muscle.
- Different types of exercises work different parts of the body.
- Too much weight training can hurt performance.

It's a good idea to have an adult present when you do weight training.

4

Get Enough Sleep for Recovery

Getting a proper amount of sleep is important to any healthy lifestyle. But for athletes, it can be even more important.

A lack of sleep has many negative effects. It can decrease both physical and mental abilities. To play your best, it's important to be in top physical form. That means getting the right amount of sleep.

Stanford University researchers did a study on the men's basketball team. Researchers asked players to sleep more than usual. Instead of getting 6.5 hours of sleep per night, players got 8.5 hours. With the extra two hours of sleep, players made more baskets. Every person is different. But sleep can make a big impact.

A normal person should get seven to nine hours of sleep per night.

Having a bedtime routine can help you get to sleep faster.

An athlete may need up to an hour more. This doesn't mean you need to go to bed earlier. Even a nap can

help. Sleep does more than help you prepare. It also helps you recover. Sleep helps the body repair itself after exercise.

13.7
Percent the Stanford basketball team's shooting improved after players got more sleep.

- Lack of sleep makes physical activity more difficult.
- Studies have proven more sleep improves performance.
- Sleep also helps the body recover after exercise.
- Naps help recovery as well.

THE GAME DAY NAP

Many NBA players believe in the power of the nap. The NBA season has 82 games. There are also lots of long road trips. That means players' bodies take a beating. Many players take a nap on game day to recharge. Former league MVP Derrick Rose naps for three hours!

Diet Matters All the Time

People need energy no matter what they're doing. When playing sports, the body needs even more energy. Food is what gives the body energy. Eating a balanced diet is one of the best ways to stay healthy. It can also improve athletic performance.

Carbohydrates, or carbs, are in foods made from grain. These foods include pasta and bread. They are high in vitamins and minerals. They also provide high amounts of energy. That's why runners often eat a lot of carbs before races. It's also helpful to eat carbs during and after exercise. They help restore energy that the body just used up.

Protein helps build muscle. It's also an energy source after the body has burned all those carbs.

Pasta makes a great meal on the day of an athletic event.

Beans are very high in protein.

Protein does not build muscle on its own. Protein builds muscle when combined with exercise and weight training. But too much protein can turn into fat. Athletes need only a little more protein than the average person.

Don't forget to stay hydrated. Water is essential to performing at your best. Drink two cups of water two hours before exercising. That will start your body off with the right amount of fluid. During exercise, drink one-half cup every 15 or 20 minutes. Keep drinking during your cooldown.

24
Ounces of fluid you should drink for every pound of body weight lost during exercise.

- Athletes need diets higher in carbohydrates and protein.
- Carbs provide energy.
- Protein builds and rebuilds muscle.
- Water is also important while exercising.

THINK ABOUT IT

What are some of your favorite foods? Are these part of a diet for an athlete? Why or why not? What changes could you make to improve your diet?

Yoga and Stretching Increase Strength and Flexibility

Many sports involve repetitive motions. These motions can overwork the same muscles. And that can lead to injury. Yoga uses these muscles in a different way. Yoga involves a series of poses and stretches. It can heal the body and improve performance. It increases flexibility and the range of motion of joints.

Take strong, deep breaths while doing yoga. This increases the body's breathing ability. And that has a benefit in sports. Getting more oxygen while playing sports can improve muscle function.

Yoga is a low-impact workout, so it isn't very stressful on your joints.

8.4 million

Number of different yoga poses.

- Yoga is a system of exercise focused on stretching.
- Yoga builds strength and flexibility.
- It can help athletes breathe better and take in more oxygen.
- It builds strength without additional weights.

YOGA IN PRO SPORTS

Yoga is becoming more popular with pro athletes. The New York Giants football team started using yoga instruction in 2001. More than one-quarter of all pro basketball players do yoga. In 2009, the Los Angeles Clippers became the first team to hire a full-time yoga instructor.

That means athletes can perform longer before feeling tired.

Some movements in yoga are very small. This helps an athlete become aware of the slightest movements. When doing specific movements, it helps to be able to make adjustments to technique.

Yoga builds strength without weights. In yoga, all you lift is yourself. But that is enough resistance to get stronger. Yoga requires a strong sense of balance. And that can help on the field.

A tiny change in a golf swing could mean a more accurate or longer shot.

15

Balance Training Helps the Body Move

Several systems control the body's sense of balance. Your brain works together with your muscles and nerves. This helps you to stay upright and make smooth movements. Good balance lowers your risk of injury. It can also help improve performance.

In many sports, good balance is a requirement. An obvious example is gymnastics. Athletes perform skills on the balance beam. But balance is important in many other sports as well. Hockey skates have thin blades that players balance on. Players skate by shifting weight from one blade to another. Golf is another sport that involves weight transfer. A golfer throws his weight forward to hit the ball farther. Balance in golf means a more accurate shot.

Balance training may start with exercises on stable ground. From there, the same exercises may move to an uneven

A balance beam is only 3.9 inches (10 cm) wide.

Studies show that hockey players with good balance can skate faster.

surface. This may be a board with a round bottom. Balance is also more difficult with limited vision. So as athletes improve, they may close their eyes to make the exercise harder.

Movement and activity are key parts of balance training. Throwing and catching while balancing helps the body get used to those activities. Balance training is not a replacement for other types of workouts. But it can be an effective addition to a training program.

1.6
Centimeters (0.6 inches) in increased vertical leap by athletes who went through a 10-week balance-training course.

- Balance training can help reduce injury risk and improve performance.
- Some sports require good balance, such as gymnastics.
- Balance increases performance in other sports, including hockey and golf.
- Balance training involves progressively more difficult activities.

17

Cardio Training Improves Movement and Stamina

The heart powers the body. Having a healthy heart can give an athlete the edge when it matters. And cardio training is one of the best ways to strengthen the heart.

Running, biking, and swimming are all cardio workouts. Many types of exercise involve stopping and starting. But cardio involves long and continuous exercise. It can be high impact, such as running. It can also be low impact, such as swimming.

Cardio is great for building endurance. Having good endurance helps an athlete perform longer without getting tired. When you're tired, your movements break down. You won't be as precise. A cardio workout helps athletes perform at their best throughout the entire

Swimming is a great workout because it's good for your heart and easy on your joints.

Biking is a fun cardio workout that you can do with friends.

event. Cardio helps muscles become better at taking in oxygen. That means they'll stay strong and recover quickly.

Cardio is not specific to any one sport. But there are ways to specialize your workout for your particular sport. For example, alternating between fast running and walking can prepare you for sports like football. This is called interval training. It helps your body be prepared to spring into action after periods of not moving.

Cardio is also excellent for weight loss. Athletes often use cardio to lose a couple pounds of fat. After 20 minutes of cardio, the body begins to burn fat. Twenty minutes of cardio exercise three or more times a week can help keep you in top shape.

8
Number of weeks after which most people start seeing improvement from cardio training.

- Cardio training works out the heart.
- Running and biking are examples of cardio.
- Cardio builds endurance so athletes don't tire as quickly.
- Cardio also helps people burn fat and lose weight.

Safety Comes First

You won't be able to play your best if you're not on the field. An injury can do more than take you out of a game. It can also affect your future performance. It might prevent you from training. Some injuries are just bad luck. But there are some steps you can take to minimize your risk.

Some sports use more equipment than others. Whether it's a full suit of pads or just some running shoes, your equipment should fit properly. If your pads are too big, they won't fully protect you. If your shoes don't fit, you could sprain an ankle. Equipment should also be in good condition so that it won't fail.

Football is a sport that has lots of safety equipment.

It's important to wear a helmet every time you ride a bike.

One injury that isn't as easy to see is a concussion. This is an injury to your brain. It's caused by getting hit in the head. Sometimes the symptoms may be small, such as dizziness. But if you hit your head, get it checked out right away. Playing with a concussion can lead to serious injuries. Concussions can happen in any sport. Athletes who play contact sports, such as football and hockey, should be extra careful.

33
Percent of concussions among high school athletes that happen at practice.

- Injuries can take you out of the game and affect future performance.
- Any equipment you wear should fit well.
- Learn to recognize the signs of concussions.
- Stop playing if you think you may have a concussion.

CONCUSSIONS IN THE NFL

Football is a sport with a high concussion rate. In 2013, the National Football League (NFL) created a set of rules on dealing with these injuries. Staff members learned about watching for the signs of concussions. If a player is suspected of having a concussion, trainers perform a series of tests. They keep the player out of the game if necessary.

21

Technology Can Track Progress

Athletes are always looking to get an edge on the competition. Having the latest technology can help.

Watches and bracelets can measure heart rate or calories burned. Athletes can then see how they measure up to where they should be. These wearables give instant results and help athletes improve.

Many people carry smartphones everywhere. They have apps to help you keep track of your fitness. You can access historic data and diet plans. You can also upload this information to a computer.

Some athletes use video to spot poor technique. Coaches can see the videos and offer tips. Players can even review video of themselves while the event is still going on. They can fix their mistakes before the game is over.

Video has been very useful in fast-paced sports like skiing and luge. Luge sleds travel down the ice very quickly. Even a tiny mistake can mean the end of a race. These mistakes are difficult to see at regular speed. But with video, they can be slowed down.

Watches can help runners track their improvements over time.

285 million

Number of wearables estimated to be in use by 2017.

- Technology plays a big role in helping athletes get better.
- Wearables help track progress and set goals.
- Smartphone apps can track many parts of your workout program.
- Video review is instant and can show mistakes.

THE TOUR DE FRANCE AT HOME

The Tour de France bicycle race is one of the toughest tests in sports. Now, fans can try it themselves. The ProForm Le Tour de France bike can download real maps from around the world. The bike simulates going up or down hills by tilting up or down. Riders can even change gears.

Some luge sleds can go 90 miles per hour (145 km/h).

Use the Latest in Equipment

The newest equipment won't turn an average athlete into an all-star. But it can give athletes an edge. Advanced equipment is one reason why records are broken.

Equipment today is lighter than ever. Tennis rackets are also stronger than ever. Stronger materials allow the racket's head to be bigger. This allows faster and more accurate shots. Golf has had similar improvements. Clubs today are made of light metals. That lets athletes swing much faster. And faster swings result in longer shots.

Modern tennis rackets are much larger than the ones people used in the mid-1900s.

Many golf clubs are made of a material called graphite.

Swimming is another sport that has benefitted from new equipment. At the 2008 Summer Olympics, many swimmers wore a suit called the Speedo LZR. This suit smoothed out the body. That helped swimmers glide through the water. The suit was very successful. More than 40 world records were set at that Olympics. Many swimming competitions soon banned the suit. People said it gave an unfair advantage to those who wore it.

Technology also plays a role in the design of equipment. Designs are now done on computers. That means the equipment can be tested before being made in real life. This helps researchers design better products.

117

Average serve speed, in miles per hour (188 km/h), of Novak Djokovic at the 2015 US Open tennis tournament.

- The newest equipment can mean an edge over the competition.
- Equipment has become lighter and stronger.
- Sports such as tennis and golf have seen more powerful shots.
- New equipment is often designed on computers.

IT TAKES TALENT, TOO

Today's hockey sticks are made of strong, light materials. Slap shots typically travel 100 miles per hour (161 km/h). But the latest equipment doesn't always mean the fastest shot. Former National Hockey League (NHL) player Al MacInnis won the Hardest Shot competition several times. And he did it with an old-fashioned wooden stick.

25

New Training Technology Can Change the Game

Sports have changed a lot in the last 100 years. In another 100 years, sports will probably change even more. How will future athletes improve their performance? A few methods are already under development.

Motion-capture is the electronic recording of a person's movements. It is often used to make movies and video games. But it could also be used to track athletes' movements. Today, a pitcher might review video of herself throwing. In the future, motion-capture might be able to spot where she went wrong.

Scientists continue to learn more about the human body. And their findings could affect sports. One day, athletes may be able to get diet and workout recommendations geared specifically for them. Athletes would know exactly what their bodies

Pro basketball player Wesley Johnson wears a motion-capture suit for the making of a video game.

20

Years that virtual reality for football use has been in development.

- Many training technologies are in development.
- Motion-capture technology can show if an athlete is performing a task correctly.
- Individual workouts can be based on a person's unique body.
- Special glasses force athletes to anticipate movement.

THINK ABOUT IT

Athletes today have all sorts of training techniques available to them. How do you think athletes trained back in the 1800s?

needed. This knowledge would help them perform their best.

In football, wide receivers may wear a special pair of glasses when training. These glasses block out the light every second or so. When a pass is thrown, the receiver is blind for a moment. He can't watch the ball the whole way. That forces him to anticipate where the ball will go. Over time, the receiver may develop instincts that help in game situations.

Football is one of the many sports in which athletes are using new technology to get an edge on opponents.

Fact Sheet

- People have played sports for thousands of years. The ancient Greeks valued sports and exercise. They began the Olympic Games nearly 3,000 years ago. The first recorded Olympic Games in 776 BCE featured running as the only sport.

- When not training for a specific sport, exercise has many benefits to general health. It increases strength and decreases the risk of some illnesses. But exercise needs are different for everybody. A workout program should be tailored to the individual and to what he or she is capable of.

- According to the President's Council on Fitness, Sports, and Nutrition, only one in three children are active every day. Just 28 percent of Americans over the age of six are regularly active. More than 78 million adults and approximately 12.5 million people in the United States are obese. Sports are a great and fun way to get active.

- The President's Council recommends that children between the ages of six and 17 should get 60 minutes or more of exercise per day. This exercise should be moderate to intense physical activity like walking, biking, or playing basketball or soccer. As part of the daily activity, children should do muscle- and bone-strengthening activities three times per week. This includes push-ups, weight lifting, or jumping rope.

Glossary

gymnastics
A sport in which participants demonstrate strength and flexibility through a series of exercises.

joint
The bending point of one of the body's limbs.

luge
An ice sport in which participants sled down a course.

oxygen
One of the gases humans need to breathe.

slap shot
A type of very fast shot in ice hockey.

smartphone
A type of cellular phone with functions similar to a computer.

sprain
An injury to the tissue surrounding a joint, such as an ankle.

wide receiver
A player in football whose main duty is to catch passes.

For More Information

Books

Sjonger, Rebecca. *Do Your Bit to be Physically Fit!* New York: Crabtree, 2016.

Sjonger, Rebecca. *Hop, Throw, and Play: Build Your Skills Every Day!* New York: Crabtree, 2016.

Stuckey, Rachel. *Be a Force on the Field: Skills, Drills, and Plays.* New York: Crabtree, 2016.

Visit 12StoryLibrary.com

Scan the code or use your school's login at **12StoryLibrary.com** for recent updates about this topic and a full digital version of this book. Enjoy free access to:

- Digital ebook
- Breaking news updates
- Live content feeds
- Videos, interactive maps, and graphics
- Additional web resources

Note to educators: Visit 12StoryLibrary.com/register to sign up for free premium website access. Enjoy live content plus a full digital version of every 12-Story Library book you own for every student at your school.

Index

About the Author

Todd Kortemeier is a writer from Minneapolis, Minnesota. He is a graduate of the University of Minnesota's School of Journalism & Mass Communication. He has authored many books for young people.

READ MORE FROM 12-STORY LIBRARY

Every 12-Story Library book is available in many formats. For more information, visit 12StoryLibrary.com.